Beautiful BEDROOMS

Design Inspirations from the World's Leading Inns and Hotels

Tina Skinner

Schiffer Publishing Ltd

4880 Lower Valley Road, Atglen, PA 19310 USA

Library of Congress Cataloging-in-Publication Data

Beautiful bedrooms : design inspirations fromthe world's leading inns
and hotels.
p. cm.
ISBN 0-7643-1461-0
1. Bedrooms. 2. Interior decoration. 3. Hotels--Decoration--Influence.
I. Schiffer Publishing Ltd.
NJ2117.B4 B37 2001
747.77--dc21
2001003759

Front cover:*Courtesy of Applewood Inn & Restaurant, Cumberland Falls Bed
and Breakfast Inn, Five Gables Inn & Spa, and Sampson Eagon Inn.*
Back cover: *Courtesy of Hotel Le Bristol and Applewood Inn & Restaurant.*
Title page: *Courtesy of Hennessey House.*

Designed by Bonnie M. Hensley
Cover design by Bruce M. Waters
Type set in Zurich BT

ISBN: 0-7643-1461-0
Printed in China

Published by Schiffer Publishing Ltd.
4880 Lower Valley Road
Atglen, PA 19310
Phone: (610) 593-1777; Fax: (610) 593-2002
E-mail: Schifferbk@aol.com
Please visit our web site catalog at **www.schifferbooks.com**
We are always looking for people to write books on new and related
subjects. If you have an idea for a book please contact us at the above
address.

This book may be purchased from the publisher.
Include $3.95 for shipping.
Please try your bookstore first.
You may write for a free catalog.

In Europe, Schiffer books are distributed by
Bushwood Books
6 Marksbury Ave.
Kew Gardens
Surrey TW9 4JF England
Phone: 44 (0) 20 8392-8585; Fax: 44 (0) 20 8392-9876
E-mail: Bushwd@aol.com
Free postage in the U.K., Europe; air mail at cost.

Dedication

Courtesy of Villa D'Este.

This book is dedicated to a wonderful person who has the bulkiest collection I've ever known – she collects bed sets. This woman can't pass through the linen department without falling in love with comforters, their matching bed skirts, and pillow shams, and maybe the curtains to match, not to mention the sheets. As a result, she can change her bed like her dresses. Fortunately, she has a home big enough to hide away those sets not in use.

This is for my dear Aunt Shirley, who has also been one of my biggest fans. And to Cousin Matt, too, who's trying to keep her out of the department stores!

ACKNOWLEDGMENTS

I love working with the hospitality industry, for reasons made obvious simply by its name! It has been a great pleasure learning about the many inns, hotels, and bed and breakfasts that supplied images for this book. These images showcase the work of a very house-proud breed of people; people who want to take in strangers and make them comfortable and happy; who work to make guests feel they've been pampered and have stayed in the very lap of luxury. They pay attention to the details of their guest rooms, with an eye toward style, comfort, and a feeling that one is at home.

CONTENTS

Cumberland Falls Bed and Breakfast Inn.

INTRODUCTION

Here it is, the room where you spend a good third of your life, albeit asleep. This room is at the very heart of our love lives, where our last endearments are shared after lights out, cuddled under quilts and soft sheets. Our children invade the bedroom for a comforting snuggle, or reassurance after a bad dream that the world is a safe place. It's also the place where we spend quality time with ourselves, reflecting on our own reflection and grooming our self-image, whether rushing to get ready for work, or primping and perfecting as we prepare for a party or date.

Our bedroom is our most secure room. We keep our treasures here: our jewelry, our wallets, our favorite family portraits. Perhaps this is because this room is the least likely to be invaded by strangers, or perhaps it is crucial to truly restful sleep that we be nestled amidst our personal wealth.

Besides family, the bedroom rarely observes outsiders. Only our closest friends are invited to enter, to share private thoughts, make comments on the latest wardrobe additions, or to borrow them. Once in a while, however, the room is invaded. When we host a party, the bedroom is where we create a great mound of coats. At the end of the festivities, the guests are sent in to pick up their wraps, and to take home an image of this room as their final impression of our house.

Decorating the bedroom is a luxury in which we indulge. The bedroom is a place where we can get silly, erotic, or outrageous. Bedrooms are great places to let the imagination soar, to let go with a jungle

Morning arrives and invites a sleeping occupant outdoors. *Courtesy of Applewood Inn & Restaurant.*

Photo © Mark Darley

All eyes on the snack, and who wouldn't sneak off for a bite here amidst this mix of three very friendly colors: sunny yellow, hunter green, and crisp white. *Courtesy of Lilac Inn.*

theme, or show off a doll collection. You can paint trees on the walls, or mount birdhouses on bedposts.

The bedroom is the room where you create a nest, lined with down and piled high with pillows. It's a retreat where you read, bathe, embrace by a warm fire, or collect your thoughts in a window seat with a view.

And when you're done, and proud of your master bedroom, and the guest rooms, and whatever other sleeping quarters you've been lucky enough to furnish, you can start charging a lot more for that fifty-cent tour.

Photo © Kindra Clineff

Opposite page:
Breakfast in bed is the ultimate imaginable luxury, curled up in satins and velvets, unconcerned with the height of the sun. *Courtesy of Old Monterey Inn.*

Simplicity at its finest: a muted blue print on toile bedspread and curtain, a subtle patina shade on the wall, allow an antique gilded frame to glow. *Courtesy of The Merrion Dublin.*

Textiles are the sensual furnishings of bedrooms, the sheets and blankets we wrap ourselves in, the coverlets that warm us, the pillows and headboards that let us lean on them. *Courtesy of Hotel Bel-Air.*

9

Chapter 1

COZY RETREATS

Here's that nest where you snuggle, bundle, or spread out. Secure and private. A quiet nook where a book is savored. A fire warms you, or a hot tub does the job. Most importantly, it's a magic place where cares float away and you surrender yourself to dreams. Courtesy of Applewood Inn & Restaurant.

This room gains grace from its minimalism: a few impressive, well crafted pieces like the headboard, the wardrobe, and a lovely lamp ; and a window framed by arched shades and simple blinds and drapes. *Courtesy of Casa Del Mar Inn*.

The cork has been popped, the bed turned down, the slippers set out. All is well with the world, and it's time to put all cares away for the night. *Courtesy of The Peninsula New York*.

Fall foliage inspired this warm print, color-keyed to dyes used in the Oriental carpet. *Courtesy of The Veranda Inn.*

Before sleep, a little light reading or a soothing cup of tea with conversation. After awakening, an invigorating brew. All in the comfort of a private little nook off the bedroom. *Courtesy of A Victorian on the Bay.*

Wonderful antiques are properly showcased in this room, each unique piece allowed to shine against a neutral wallpaper print. *Courtesy of Hennessey House.*

A big floral motif on bed and canopy repeats colors found in historic paintings hanging on the wall. Note that the picture hangers were treated with the same green watered-silk satin as the canopy and the upholstered chair in the foreground. *Courtesy of Monmouth Plantation.*

Blue and gold work together for layers of texture. A crocheted bed cover adds texture and softens the effect of crisp baby blue. *Courtesy of Monmouth Plantation.*

A cottage atmosphere is created using wicker and cheerful peach tones. *Courtesy of Birchwood Inn*

A bed bedecked in hand-sewn quilt and embroidered linens lies nestled below a wonderful roof line, replete with skylights. *Courtesy of The Log House & Homestead.*

This whirlpool tub for two puts soakers in a bay window with mountain vistas. *Courtesy of Franklin Manor Bed & Breakfast.*

A seating area and a hot tub take advantage of the lower spaces under a sloping wood-beam ceiling, without blocking the light (or mountain view) from a wall of windows. *Courtesy of Franklin Manor Bed & Breakfast*.

A whirlpool tub was built into its own lush pavilion in a corner, competing for attention with a fireplace bedecked with greens and lights for Christmas. *Courtesy of The Hillcrest Inn.*

A warm brocade tapestry forms a backdrop behind the bed, dramatized by draperies that continue over a wall of windows. With the shades drawn, the room is lit by a wood-burning fireplace set in a decorative ceramic tile surround. *Courtesy of Old Monterey Inn.*

Photo © Jay Graham

Fox hunting scenes circle the room on wallpaper border and in frames. A woodstove invites two people to cozy up and share their stories of the chase. *Courtesy of Hennessey House.*

A glorious net of lace crowns a curve-top canopy over this bed, dominating the room. A handsome Windsor chair faces the brick fireplace. *Courtesy of Rabbit Hill Inn.*

A couch is tucked neatly under the window, transforming one end of the room into a seating area. *Courtesy of The Mark.*

A rose lover brought the garden indoors to this room. *Courtesy of Birchwood Inn*.

The clean lines in this room are deceiving, seeming so casual. Yet a lot of thought went into the placement of the furnishings to achieve this elegant effect. *Courtesy of Bellevue Club Hotel.*

After a leisurely soak in warm bubbles, the bed is just a tumble away. This is a space-saving plan, and wonderfully romantic. Room darkening shades make it possible to take a midday nap. *Courtesy of The Mill Brook.*

Rough hewn beams and an expanse of window are this room's architectural charms. To compete with them, the chairs and bedspread are adorned bold red. *Courtesy of The Lodge.*

Earth tones give a warm glow to this room. From the sexy stretch of chaise lounge to the stuffed and upholstered headboard, this room is all about lounging with a good book. *Courtesy of Hotel Jerome.*

A good book is one of the best ways to unwind, and bookshelves are always well worn in the bedroom. Fluff up the pillows, turn on the reading light, and you're all set. *Courtesy of The Peninsula New York*

Here is a room of rich contrast: ornate floral wall, window, and bed coverings vs. simple wood furnishings. *Courtesy of Hotel Byblos.*

This designer worked repeating colors and motifs into the room, tying together golds and blues in the textiles, mocha furniture finishes with picture frames and pillow fringe. The result is an elegant symmetry. *Courtesy of Hôtel Plaza Athénée.*

A lot is made of this small room, brightened by sunny yellow walls and cheerful floral linens. A rich, dark finish on the furnishings adds elegance to the atmosphere. This is a lamp-lover's room, with three unique and elegant lighting units – two in glass and one in brass. *Courtesy of The Madison Hotel.*

Choosing matching textiles and wallpapers makes a room feel padded; swaddled against outside noise and distractions. Beyond, an enclosed balcony has been finished in contrasting whites. *Courtesy of Hôtel Plaza Athénée.*

A starred coverlet tops a skirt of stripes, which are paralleled in curtains and the upholstered chairs. The chaise lounge sits bathed in light, forming an attractive window seat. *Courtesy of Hôtel Plaza Athénée*

Chapter 2

AMAZING SPACES

Sometimes we need to spread out before we snuggle in. Sitting areas are, once again, being incorporated in architect's plans for new homes. Many is the new master bedroom that is not one but two rooms, interconnected. It's a special retreat for master and mistress, or the most intimate of family gathering spaces. It may be where we exercise our bodies, or merely our minds with a good book. Whatever the function, the space creates a special challenge for the home decorator: furnishing two spaces that work together. Courtesy of Hotel Le Bristol.

The elegance of a Victorian music conservatory inspired this room, where one might muse by the fire or compose a romantic encounter. *Courtesy of The Inn at 410*.

It is becoming increasingly popular to build two-room master bedrooms in today's new homes. Here is a wonderful example of how the second chamber can become a quiet retreat for private conversation and relaxation. *Courtesy of Hotel Byblos*.

Richard Weston Photography

Shot from the breakfast nook, one looks out over an expansive spread of room. Eye catchers include a towering steel bed frame and a wonderful antique steamer trunk. The palest of pink accents adds interest to a room in many shades of white. *Courtesy of Lilac Inn.*

Symmetry adds crisp elegance to this sitting area and the bedchamber beyond. All things are equal and in balance. *Courtesy of Hotel Byblos.*

This room is rich in color, with bold striped textiles on the bed and windows, and a wallpaper with oversized sprays of floral arrangements. Adding to the mix, a wonderful wood floor, dating from 1885, shows off its colors. The room is big enough to accommodate this profusion of coloring, and includes two seating areas where one can read, rock, or converse around a fire. *Courtesy of Birchwood Inn.*

Here's a hangout of a bedroom, complete with writing desk, a fire-lit conversation area, and a window seat retreat. *Courtesy of Birchwood Inn*

Looking out from beneath a draped canopy bed, one sees the attractions this room has for someone not yet sleepy. Both bed and couch are positioned to take in a view out the window, as well as a roaring fire. A painted insert graces a door panel, leading out to a private sundeck. *Courtesy of Rabbit Hill Inn.*

A white bed with lacy wrought iron headboard beckons beyond a bright antechamber. *Courtesy of The Chesterfield Palm Beach.*

A fireplace with wonderful wood-work surrounding it competes for attention with an impressive canopy bed. *Courtesy of Litchfield Plantation*.

A barrier wall forms an entry hall for this massive bedroom, and creates a private nook for the bed. Matching textiles tie seating area and bedroom together. *Courtesy of The Mark*.

A voluminous wall hanging frames the headboard. More yardage was used for the window treatment as well as the bed coverlet and skirt. *Courtesy of Hotel Le Bristol.*

A loft looks down on this charming green room. Golden molding behind the bed accentuates the ceiling height. *Courtesy of The Merrion Dublin.*

A dark finish on wood furnishings imparts a sense of importance, of stateliness. Rich reds and greens in the upholstery and window dressings add to this timeless effect. *Courtesy of The Lancaster.*

Pink in the architectural and textile details give this room a feminine feeling, with tropical touches in the wall art. *Courtesy of The Chesterfield Palm Beach.*

Green and gold textiles add warmth to a room rich in formal furnishings. *Courtesy of Hotel de L'Europe.*

A subtle hint of rose runs through the cream colors in this room. *Courtesy of Hotel Le Bristol.*

35

Paint on exposed brick adds texture to a cool white room. A window alcove becomes a quiet nook for bedtime reading or conversation. *Courtesy of Sanctuary on Camelback Mountain.*

Positioned in the corner, a canopied bed allows its occupant a view beyond the balcony, of a sitting area, and of the writing table that is also mirrored on the wall. *Courtesy of Kahala Mandarin Oriental.*

Queen Anne style furnishings give this spacious bedroom its classic elegance. *Courtesy of The Pierre Hotel.*

The owners have christened this room "Pheasant Dreams" for the theme of the artwork and decor. *Courtesy of Hennessey House.*

Architecture adds so much to a room. Here the slope of the roof is interrupted by fireplace and hallway. *Courtesy of Hennessey House.*

A bedroom is a wonderful place to showcase an eclectic collection. Here, equestrian-related antiques have earned this room the its reputation as the "Bridle Suite." *Courtesy of Hennessey House.*

A bold plum paint contrasts with white on the generous moldings, and complements stained glass windows. A generous windowed alcove is home to a white wrought-iron bed framed by a swag of lace. *Courtesy of The Dupont at the Circle.*

This room stays understated to show off a tile floor with wonderful, hand-painted tile designs. Cool white walls reflect the brilliant sunshine in this tropical resort. *Courtesy of Vila Vita Parc.*

Enormous drapes can be dropped to separate the sleeping and sitting areas. Rich green brocade contrasts with romantic red velvet upholstery. *Courtesy of Villa D'Este.*

Spectacular space stretches away from this bedroom, with a private sitting area crowned by a painted dome overhead. The painted floral and ribbon motif is carried throughout the room, in the textiles and the wallpaper. A sky blue carpet underlines all. *Courtesy of Palisades Bed & Breakfast.*

A private sitting room and bedchamber are elaborately draped in blue and gold brocade, complete with tasseled fringe. The effect is regal. *Courtesy of Monmouth Plantation.*

Striking contrasts of cream, taupe,
espresso, rich mahogany, and stainless
steel create a truly dramatic impression.
Courtesy of Fifteen Beacon.

Teak wood parquet flooring, wooden beams, and a simple wooden frame define the clean, Asian style of this room. A wonderful natural fiber backdrop behind the bed becomes artwork for the wall. An artful wicker chair and ottoman take care of the decor on another wall. *Courtesy of The Oberoi.*

An unusual bed frame in smooth cement offers options in bedside seating, as well as a place to do one's toenails or set a drink. Besides being practical, the effect is architectural, mirroring the fireplace surround and the sofa in an open-air sitting room beyond a drawn-back, filmy curtain. *Courtesy of Las Ventanas al Paraiso.*

A blend of beige tones softens this sumptuous room, drawing attention to detailing in the tailoring of window and wall hangings, the fine furniture that includes a gilded headboard, and the crystal lamps. *Courtesy of Mandarin Oriental Hyde Park.*

Glimmering gold was worked into this room to underline the lavish expanses of inviting resting spots. *Courtesy of Mandarin Oriental Hyde Park.*

A contemporary design, with simple lines, creates stunning effect. A partial wood wall divides sleeping and entertaining areas. *Courtesy of Mandarin Oriental, Hotel du Rhône.*

A daybed lies at the center of a spacious room, ready for daydreams. *Courtesy of Begawan Giri Estate.*

Chapter 3

BRIGHT INTERIORS

The tendency is to think of bedrooms as the dark place where we close our eyes. Lucky is the homeowner whose boudoir also beckons by day, with streams of sunlight to warm the heart. A place where eyes stay wide open and daydreams are born. Here, like a present tied with a pretty ribbon of post and beam, a decorative canopy tops a bed dressed in antique white linens and an inviting window seat commands a view over an acre of English gardens. Courtesy of Old Monterey Inn.

Soft whites and beiges blend for a comforting atmosphere. *Courtesy of The Peninsula New York.*

Antique furnishings give this room its one-of-a-kind ambience. French doors on both sides of the bed open for a cross-breeze and access to a private garden patio. *Courtesy of Hotel Bel-Air.*

A wonderful lattice headboard of wrought iron gives this room its unique character. *Courtesy of The Equinox.*

Soft cotton frocks, a white rattan headboard, and pale blue gingham are a recipe for sweet dreams. *Courtesy of On the Banks of the Everglades.*

A comfortable Arts and Crafts hideaway features a massive oak bed, rocking chair, and sofa. Stenciling in shades of green, rust, and copper brings the garden indoors. *Courtesy of Oakland House Seaside Resort.*

A pile of silk pillows is ready to prop you up after a hard day in the city. *Courtesy of The Peninsula New York.*

The sparkly blue scene beyond is snow-covered pines, contrasting with the warm, golden furnishings in this simple yet elegant bedroom suite. *Courtesy of Hotel Byblos.*

Two rooms become one, with partial walls to separate the sleeping area from a sitting area and private balcony. Molding is used to create panels, and allow for two-tone walls. *Courtesy of Villa D'Este.*

Towering windows are flanked by elegant swaths of drapery, accenting the grandeur of high ceilings. *Courtesy of Bellevue Club Hotel.*

The stripes in the curtains parallel the balcony rail and the ocean horizon beyond. *Courtesy of Cheeca Lodge.*

Simplicity and sparing furnishings allow elegant details to stand out. This room emphasizes contrasts in shape, from the modern arches in window and headboard to the squares of pillows and windowpanes. *Courtesy of Cheeca Lodge.*

A paneled wall divides sleeping and sitting areas in an expansive suite. Masculine gray and black linens are softened with natural tones. *Courtesy of Le Meridien Sydney.*

Louvered wood panels add warmth to a city studio room and create private areas between a bedroom and adjacent sitting area. *Courtesy of The Oriental Singapore.*

Crisp shades of white contrast with earthen tones and Asian forms. *Courtesy of Gaige House Inn.*

By day this boudoir becomes a sunroom; a warmly inviting place to take a nap. *Courtesy of Gaige House Inn.*

Architecture is your frame, the furnishings your canvas; use texture and color as your brushes and paints. . .

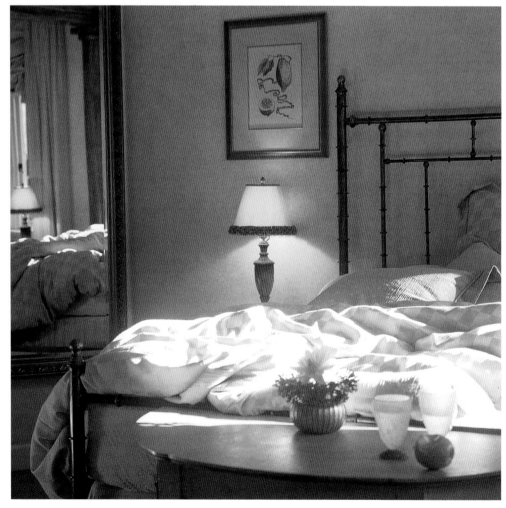

And then you mix them. *Courtesy of Hotel Sausalito.*

A canopied bed is sumptuously sunk into a windowed alcove. Soft white lace graces a room swathed in gentle tones. *Courtesy of The Dupont at the Circle.*

Forget about time, the big mirror on the wall seems to say. This lofty hideaway is a place where cares float away in a bubbly bath or upon a thick down comforter. *Cumberland Falls Bed and Breakfast Inn*

Chapter 4

COUNTRY CHARM

An enduring decorator's theme, country — whether in the city or suburbs — typifies American style. The look is becoming more sophisticated, moving beyond the blue-and-white, beribboned farm animal themes of a decade ago. And there is no set look to evoke our farm roots now, just a self-satisfying mix of antiques, home-mades, and simple patterns. Here the effect is achieved using knotty pine furnishings, quilted pillows, stripes and plaid, and a loon decoy. Courtesy of Rabbit Hill Inn.

A handcrafted quilt in the traditional Star of Bethlehem design graces an inviting bed tucked neatly under the eaves in this rooftop getaway. *Courtesy of Henley House.*

This room displays a rich Pennsylvania tradition of quilting. Amish children's clothes adorn the wall. *Courtesy of Ashton Country House.*

A cherry four-post bed, a fireplace, and inset shelving characterize this room. A bird theme originated in the wallpaper design and was carried over in a birdhouse collection and the textiles. *Courtesy of Ashton Country House*

Generous toile draperies on this canopy bed create a romantic retreat. *Courtesy of Rabbit Hill Inn.*

A brick corner unit hosts a warm wood stove and becomes the focal point of this bright room. Another nice feature is the wooden beamed ceiling with a glowing finish. *Courtesy of Joshua Grindle Inn.*

A wallpapered ceiling creates a colorful canopy in this rooftop room. A wonderful sleigh bed has been tucked under the eaves, and overstuffed for comfort. *Courtesy of Joshua Grindle Inn.*

Light blues and whites in the textiles are set against bold brown timbers and cantaloupe walls. Green wicker and wrought iron add texture. *Courtesy of Applewood Inn & Restaurant.*

Knotty wood paneling forms a warm backdrop for a red and white bed. *Courtesy of Black Forest Inn.*

This large, sunny suite has the blues: *Blue Ivy,* Van Gogh's *Starry Night*, *Grandma Battin's Garden*, and *Blue Island Party* on the walls. Beadboard wainscoting topped by blue striped wallpaper works with wicker for this room's country appeal. *Courtesy of Capitol Hill Mansion.*

The colors in a handmade quilt are echoed in the room's adornments, set against a frame of rich salmon pink. *Courtesy of Ashton Country House.*

A wonderful hooked rug marries the sunny yellow of a star quilt with the satin blue of an upholstered chair. A hand-carved dresser counts among the room's treasures, and the bedside table is an antique Singer sewing machine. *Courtesy of Birchwood Inn.*

65

A burgundy on the walls allows the white and blues of a piecework quilt to stand out in this room. A woodstove in the corner makes a reading chair all the more inviting. *Courtesy of Birchwood Inn.*

A range of wonderf[ul] reds enjoy full play i[n] this room, from th[e] French-inspired toi[le] print on the bed[-] spread, to th[e] magnificent antiqu[e] star quilt that creates [a] backdrop. *Courtesy [of] The Veranda In[n.]*

Upholstering the headboard in the same fabric as the bedspread creates a comfy feeling. A bold Wedgwood blue on the walls fills in the blanks, from floor to handsome crown moldings. *Courtesy of The Merrion Dublin.*

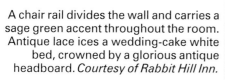

A chair rail divides the wall and carries a sage green accent throughout the room. Antique lace ices a wedding-cake white bed, crowned by a glorious antique headboard. *Courtesy of Rabbit Hill Inn.*

A wonderful lace canopy covers a four-poster bed. The rich textiles and wonderful wood floor, timber, and beams account for the room's charm. *Courtesy of Rabbit Hill Inn.*

This room was furnished with antiques from a Kansas farmhouse, including an oversized bed with stepstool. *Courtesy of Chipita Lodge.*

A massive bed frame of aspen logs dominates this Western-theme room. Cowboy boots stand as art by a dresser, and buffaloes roam on a pillowcase. Beyond, post office boxes and a mail slot from a previous incarnation of the lodge hold up a vanity. *Courtesy of Chipita Lodge.*

This room is flooded with the copper tones of sunset and the hushed greens of the surrounding forest. *Courtesy of Oakland House Seaside Resort.*

A wood-lover's dream, this paneled room includes a gorgeous wood floor and a handsome, mission-style bed. *Courtesy of Black Forest Inn.*

An elegant canopy bed and conservative upholstered chairs contrast against a rich background of floral wallpaper. The slate-colored valance and pillow shams coordinate the look. *Courtesy of Rabbit Hill Inn.*

Knotty yellow pine furnishings glow against a burgundy and green backdrop. A wonderful frosted glass light fixture hangs in the center of the room and casts the kind of glow that makes everyone look great after dark. *Courtesy of The Equinox.*

Making the most of a small room, wooden pegs take up some of the slack in storage and display beside a bed too close to the wall for a second night table. *Courtesy of The Equinox.*

White becomes an powerful accent in this room, contrasted against the brick red walls, real brick fireplace surround, and rich colors in plaid print and Oriental carpet. *Courtesy of Birchwood Inn.*

Teapots and roses adorn this lush room, lavishly decorated in high Victorian style. *Courtesy of The Inn at 410.*

Vivid yellow sunflowers and brilliant sky blue were woven together to bring a sunny summer landscape indoors. *Courtesy of The Inn at 410.*

Bent willow furniture, primitive antiques, and a pine tree border bring the peace and serenity of Northern Arizona's ponderosa forest to this room. *Courtesy of The Inn at 410.*

The canopy bed, unique pottery basin, and Mexican furnishings give this room a Southwestern feel. *Courtesy of Chipita Lodge.*

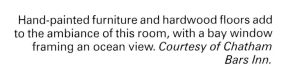

A painted headboard, print wallpaper, and built-in shelves give this room practical, natural appeal. *Courtesy of Woodstock Inn & Resort.*

Hand-painted furniture and hardwood floors add to the ambiance of this room, with a bay window framing an ocean view. *Courtesy of Chatham Bars Inn.*

Chapter 5

PERIOD PIECES

A treasured collection of antiques may inspire your period room; or maybe it's a place where you memorialize an ancestor. Maybe you simply yearn for a simpler time, for your own Tara, or the splendor of a Victorian parlor. It's not old-fashioned to look back when decorating. In fact, it increases in vogue as a new generation seeks to connect itself with the past. Courtesy of Captain Nickerson Inn.

This beautifully hand-turned poplar bed is a circa 1890 piece from southwestern Virginia, with a hand-tied, arched canopy. *Courtesy of Sampson Eagon Inn.*

The most has been made of antiques in this room, from the primitive portraits on the wall, to a wonderful four-poster bed. A fireplace surround is a lovely focal point, and beside it an old china cabinet serves as bookshelf and dresser, tucked in the nook created by the chimney. *Courtesy of Joshua Grindle Inn.*

A unique, handcrafted bed frame and octagonal side table characterize this room. *Courtesy of Cincinnati's Weller Haus.*

An amazing Victorian-era headboard holds court in this room, crowned in velvet and flanked by marble topped table and vanity. *Cumberland Falls Bed and Breakfast Inn.*

A colorful quilt and an elaborate antique headboard characterize this room. *Courtesy of The Columns on Alamo.*

This is a commanding headboard, stretching over seven feet in height. Tonal variations in the hand-carved moldings and twin oval insets add interest. *Courtesy of Edgewood Farm.*

Three layers of lace form a backdrop to a bed draped in soft satin. *Courtesy of Waterloo Country Inn.*

An antique coverlet in yellow and orange tones grabs the eye, while lace curtains frame the handsome, wrought iron bed, the centerpiece in a room furnished with antiques. *Courtesy of Cincinnati's Weller Haus.*

Arts and Crafts style furnishings add straightforward elegance to this large suite. *Courtesy of The Inn at 410.*

Beauty is in the details, and here much of it is white on white, in the wonderful fireplace surround and the rich matelasse bedspread. The circa 1810 Massachusetts Empire mahogany bed has an intricately carved headboard and spiral posts. The walnut wardrobe is a local piece, dating to about 1860. A period gilt mirror with original glass reflects light from the Venetian blown glass chandelier. *Courtesy of Sampson Eagon Inn.*

Decorated in the Colonial Revival style, all of the furnishings and objets d'art are the innkeeper's family heirlooms. An exceptional grouping of 17th and 18th century English and Dutch delft tiles surround the fireplace. Blue and ivory Woodridge toile du Jouy enhances the period feel of the room. *Courtesy of Sampson Eagon Inn.*

A hand-screened reproduction documentary print fabric was used in the window treatment and for curtains behind the bed to set an early 19th Century tone in this period-theme room, which is a mélange of styles in fashion during the first half of the 19th century. *Courtesy of Sampson Eagon Inn.*

A four-poster bed was draped in a print appropriate to the 19th Century furnishings. The owners paid careful attention to all of the furnishings, choosing antiques and reproduction furniture in keeping with the home's long history. *Courtesy of Philip Porcher House.*

Wood is the traditional Arts and Crafts era decorative element. Here trim, and authentic oak furnishings are stained dark green to highlight the grain produced by a living tree: a color scheme popularized in magazines circulated in 1907. *Courtesy of Oakland House Seaside Resort.*

This room enjoys a timeless elegance, with a four-poster bed and a wonderful vanity with three-panel mirror. Grecian urn lamps and a settee at the end of the bed add lovely detail. *Courtesy of The Equinox.*

Painted Oglethorpe Blue, this suite was lavished with gold and teal window tapestries, a portrait in a gilded frame, and a king canopy bed adorned in patterned gold velvet. *Courtesy of The President's Quarters.*

Roy J. Wright photographer

A four-post bed and a wonderful antique fireplace surround take center stage in a room furnished to recreate the 1800s. *Courtesy of The Inn at Irving Place.*

A crocheted coverlet
tames a shiny satin
bedspread. Above, a
matching canopy was
elaborately interwoven
with rust-colored velvet,
a design mirrored in the
window treatment
beyond. *Courtesy of*

A topping of orange sherbet and hints of lime add tropical zing to
this lacy, feminine room. *Courtesy of Monmouth Plantation.*

Chocolate wood works with cream and toffee velvets in this warm room. Amazingly wide planks fill the space between pillows and elaborate carving on the headboard. *Courtesy of Monmouth Plantation.*

A meticulous eye for matching colors keyed textiles with a wallpaper border in this room. The finish on antique furnishings is in like agreement. *Courtesy of Monmouth Plantation.*

An amazing antique bed plays a starring role in this room. A headrest was shaped from one large board on the headboard, and dentil work crowns the entire affair. *Courtesy of Monmouth Plantation.*

87

Chapter 6

EUROPEAN INFLUENCE

Our tastes in furnishings weren't invented yesterday. They were cultivated through centuries. The "finest furnishings" by definition embody the woodworking, gilding, and upholstery skills developed in Europe and exported throughout the world. And though "European design" frequently embodies the silks of China, the woods of tropical regions, and the carpets loomed in the Middle East, these furnishings were developed for a European clientele and incorporated as part of a look distinctly Western in nature. Courtesy of The Ashton.

An intricately carved, four-poster bed is lavished in rich fabrics and set against a background of navy blue wallpaper with gold bees dedicated to Napoleon and set off with a fleur-de-lis carpet. *Courtesy of The Veranda Inn.*

Honeyed golds and orange create a regal atmosphere around this expansive, king-size bed. Sage green curtains add an accent color, mirrored in the painting over the bed. *Courtesy of Hotel Vier Jahreszeiten.*

The sheen of satin adds splendor to this room, contrasted with gold tones for regal effect. The color scheme is playfully carried out, through textiles, wall finishes, and well-wrought panels on the woodwork. *Courtesy of Villa D'Este.*

Red is the color of romance, and here it is used lavishly in big curtains, ready to drop from brass rails and conceal the bedchamber. *Courtesy of Villa D'Este.*

From the timbered, arched ceiling, to the tiled floor with Oriental carpet, this room speaks of age and grace. Its beauty is in details, from the gilded mirror above a marble fireplace, to the impeccably reupholstered antique furniture. *Courtesy of Grand Hotel Excelsior Vittoria.*

Pinks and greens reflect the feminine touch that went into this room's design, illuminated by a crystal chandelier. *Courtesy of Hotel Le Bristol.*

A cavernous room is formally decorated, with choice antique pieces placed just so around the perimeter. *Courtesy of Hotel Le Bristol.*

There's a beautiful view from this window, be it outside or of oneself. This elegant room centers on its large brass bed and stone fireplace topped by gilt decorative moldings. *Courtesy of The Ritz, London.*

A marble fireplace, an antique vanity with three-panel mirror, four layers of curtains, and French provincial antique furniture: this room speaks history and opulence. *Courtesy of The Ritz, London.*

Curtains can be drawn across brass rails to cordon off a sitting area while another rests. *Courtesy of The Ritz, London.*

A chandelier and gilded moldings work with formal furnishings for a stately suite. *Courtesy of The Ritz, London.*

Golden hues create a relaxing atmosphere framed by rich moldings. An elaborate fireplace surround is the room's center-piece, topped by an oversize mirror to add sparkle, even when the fire is not lit. It is a great luxury to be able to face into the room from one's desk, instead of facing the wall. *Courtesy of Hotel Lancaster.*

Drapes form a backdrop for this bed, with the blue print also incorporated into lamp shades for a uniform look. A wall vanity creates a small work area in this limited space. *Courtesy of Hotel de L'Europe.*

This room's sweeping elegance is defined by an exotic valance and drapery behind a curvaceous headboard. A grand window and private balcony extend beyond. *Courtesy of Reid's Palace Hotel.*

The classic appeal of golden silks and fine furnishings doesn't mean one must sacrifice comfort. Here the bed is piled high with pillows, deep with down. *Courtesy of The Waldorf Towers.*

Red is a wonderful accent color, here used generously to punctuate a classic gold and cream scheme. *Courtesy of The Waldorf Towers.*

An elaborate curtain forms a backdrop behind the bed, falling in extravagant puddles at the side. When desired, the drapes can be drawn to tent the bed in a wonderful canopy of gold and red velvet. *Courtesy of The Waldorf Towers.*

97

A bed is crowned and draped for dramatic effect, all the art a wall really needs. Nevertheless, in a continuity of symmetry, matching pictures were hung above a perfect pair of bedside lamps. *Courtesy of Mandarin Oriental Hyde Park.*

The view up from the bed is most impressive, the size of this suite aside. Someone painstakingly pleated golden satin to create this amazing bed canopy. *Courtesy of Hotel Vier Jahreszeiten.*

A whimsical trompe l'oeil spread wraps this bed. Beyond, an elaborate border marks the entrance to a bubbling Jacuzzi set in a marble floor. *Courtesy of Rose Inn.*

Gold is the color of wealth, a color once reserved for China's royalty. Here is a room resplendent in rich gold and red hues, lending the atmosphere a regal air. *Courtesy of Hôtel Plaza Athénée*

Chapter 7

EXOTIC FANTASIES

Our wildest dreams transport us to faraway lands and exotic cultures. So in the room in which we are most free to indulge our dreams, it's appropriate that we feel free to decorate accordingly. The bedroom should foster romance; it should indulge our passions. It should be shrouded in mystery, or packed with fun. Courtesy of Begawan Giri Estate.

Here's a tropic bed fit for island royalty, with red carpet leading up to it and pillows for those who would sit at the foot. Hanging lanterns offer nighttime illumination. *Courtesy of Begawan Giri Estate.*

Mosquito netting envelops this bed and creates a bright spot in a soothingly dark room, a retreat from the tropic sun and heat outside. *Courtesy of Begawan Giri Estate.*

A four-poster bed is elaborately carved in tropic style, with a platform around the sleeping pad where one can perch to remove their shoes before slipping under cool sheets. *Courtesy of Begawan Giri Estate.*

An enormous platform bed lies in a room open to the elements. Sleeping outdoors is a universal fantasy, achievable only in the most comfortable of climates. *Courtesy of Begawan Giri Estate.*

The decorative elements in this room – the wallpaper border, the rug, the bed canopy – are so richly detailed that one feels as though they've stepped inside a velvet painting. *Courtesy of Monmouth Plantation.*

Working within the constraints of an enormous post and beam, this four-poster bed ties itself in with draperies that attach to the structure. Rich red and green tones give the room its classic, timeless elegance. *Courtesy of Rabbit Hill Inn.*

This room plays with the contrast between natural shapes in foliage and the geometric forms in the wicker chair cushions and the wall hanging. The bright green walls are muted by creams and darker greens in the complementary textiles. *Courtesy of L'Auberge Provencale.*

Red, the color of romance, is revealed beneath a blanket of richly tailored drapery, spotted in a throw pillow, and planted among fresh flowers. *Courtesy of Mandarin Oriental Hyde Park.*

Lighting sets the mood, and here it is dim and golden for romantic effect. *Courtesy of Bellevue Club Hotel.*

Wicker furnishings and palm fronds give this room its tropical flavor, complemented by ocean blues. *Courtesy of Cheeca Lodge.*

Rich wood trim and flooring tie together a blend of Asian textile designs in bed linens and a throw carpet. Fresh sea breezes are channeled in through window panels that rotate for 100 percent exposure. *Courtesy of Le Royal Meridien Baan Taling Ngam.*

The bedcover print and the distinct grid work on the hutch add the spice of Asia to this room.
*Mandarin Oriental * San Francisco*

A view like this makes the bedroom a magnet, so it's important to be prepared to hang out with comfortable furniture and a nook for coffee and conversation. *Courtesy of Cheeca Lodge.*

An imported bowl, an exotic pillow cover, an ornate curtain design give a worldly air to this room. *Courtesy of The Waldorf Towers.*

Asian inspirations mingle with old world furnishings for a classic fusion. *Courtesy of The Waldorf Towers.*

A crystal chandelier, tasseled tiebacks for the bed curtains, and an abundance of fresh flowers make this suite fit for a princess. *Courtesy of Mandarin Oriental Hyde Park.*

Russet wicker works with a striped bedspread and kilim-inspired upholstery on one chair. *Courtesy of The Fairmont Scottsdale Princess.*

A mosaic headboard behind you, a gilded box of treasure at your feet, and a blue sea at your fingertips on which great dreams can set sail. The bed frame and bedside tables are actually structural, built of the same cement and stucco as the walls. *Courtesy of Las Ventanas al Paraiso.*

Asian influences here include the geometric print on bedspread and pillows, and the ceramic jug of Oriental origin. Palm leaves and a billowy bed canopy add romance. *Courtesy of Kahala Mandarin Oriental.*

Exotic textiles create a worldly retreat in this expansive bedroom, softly lit by crystal chandelier. *Courtesy of Mandarin Oriental Hyde Park.*

The rounded edges on bed and room were created through the magic of a fish-eye camera lens. The magic of emerald tiles was pure chemistry in the kiln, and the tailored bedspread and valance were crafted with great care and attention. *Courtesy of Hotel Santa Caterina.*

111

Exotic textiles shroud a bed in luxury. *Courtesy of Applewood Inn & Restaurant.*

Wonderful Art Deco styling went into this unique four-poster bed. A sheepskin carpet in front of a settee offers up a cushy place for tired toes. *Cumberland Falls Bed and Breakfast Inn.*

An exotic, domed and curtained bed creates an exciting retreat, surrounded by fringe and tassels. Regency-era furnishings and decor recall a 19th century London townhouse. *Courtesy of The Lanesborough.*

Art imitates life. A wallpaper border mirrors real swags of fabric draped around his sumptuous bed canopy. *Courtesy of Monmouth Plantation.*

This suite is resplendent in black, gold, and yellow decor, a room fit for celebrities and world leaders – many of whom have slept here. *Courtesy of the Kempinski Hotel Corvinus.*

Rich gold and red tones and intricately carved, richly stained woodwork characterize this room and give it its Asian flair. The wooden feet on the floor lamps and chaise lounge are of particular interest, and draw attention to the beautiful Oriental carpet underlining the seating area. *Courtesy of The Dharmawangsa.*

Mosquito netting adds romance to an imposing, square, solid teak platform bed. This island-style room has an informal definition between indoors and out, with a wall that opens the room to the elements. A soaring bamboo ceiling adds texture and warmth. *Courtesy of The Oberoi.*

Two walls of windows can be curtained off for privacy, or thrown open for an incredible view. Inside, a cozy nest of golden textiles and fluffy pillows beckons. *Courtesy of The Pan Pacific San Francisco.*

Recessed wall nooks are lit from dramatic effect in this wonderful adobe room, where squares have been rejected in favor of Roman arches. *Courtesy of Hotel Santa Caterina.*

Chapter 8

ONE-OF-A-KIND

If you're lucky, or truly determined, you'll have a slice of architecture, or a headboard, or wardrobe chest so unique none other could possibly compare. Here unique is created with two brick walls left in their natural state. To capitalize on this structural muscle, the designer sought out a quilted spread that mirrors the wonderful walls; and gleaned other strong elements from antique shops like the wrought iron bed frame and the former window-grate that hangs on the wall; and an Adirondack chair with its old paint stripped away. Courtesy of Five Gables Inn & Spa.

An old masonry wall gives this room its atmosphere of rich textures. The wicker chair, brass bed and floor lamp, and wooden blanket chest are antiques befitting the age and stateliness of the foundation they look upon. *Courtesy of The Dupont at the Circle.*

Garden green frames a purple pansy quilt in a cheerful room warmed by woodstove. A wall of windows provides an inspiring view. *Cumberland Falls Bed and Breakfast Inn.*

This antique oak bed was a treasured auction find. A neighbor happily hand-painted the walls of roses, and the owner made the window treatments, bed skirt, and chair cover. Local Amish made the quilt. *Courtesy of The Artist's Inn & Gallery.*

Mixing rich, natural-tone textiles with wood beams creates warmth in this room. Accent pillows and a mirror carry the print's reflection throughout the room. *Courtesy of Hotel Byblos*

This room had to have color to compete with the incredible red rock views through the windows. Native American art adorns wall and stucco fireplace surround, evoking the ancient pictograph and petroglyph sites found nearby. *Courtesy of Southwest Inn at Sedona.*

Huge timbers frame a fireplace and form the centerpiece for this room. The timbers contrast starkly with the white-on-white decor, reflective of the winter scenes for which this village is famous. *Courtesy of Thurnhers Alpenhof.*

Wall sconces and a fire cast warm light on this room, decorated with an exotic collection of textiles. *The Inn at Stockbridge.*

Bright shades of orange transform this room into a cheerful hideaway. A sofa at the foot of the bed becomes a wonderful breakfast nook, for coffee, a croissant, and the morning news. *Courtesy of Hotel Byblos.*

Indian crafts, Mexican pottery, and contemporary Southwestern art complement the organic textures and muted hues of this tranquil suite. *Courtesy of The Inn at 410.*

A riot of textures and patterns evoke the excitement of a Mexican market in this festive room. *Courtesy of The Inn at 410.*

An artistically inspired room uses trompe l'oeil to expose holes in brickwork that aren't really there. The magic of an impressionistic fairy tale sets this room amidst a French countryside background of greenery and flower blossoms. *Courtesy of The Inn at 410.*

Rich details in the carved, four-poster canopy bed are matched in the accompanying bedspread and window treatments. Above, painted beams contrast with green walls. *Courtesy of Hotel Maison de Ville.*

An array of exquisite antiques, including the wooden horse in the foreground and the canopied bed with merry-go-round posts add pleasing texture and exploratory interest to this room. Another treasure is the pineapple chandelier. *Courtesy of L'Auberge Provencale.*

This room seems segregated under the diagonal grid of heavy ceiling beams. A television pops out of a cabinet and can be angled toward a viewer on either comfy couch or bed. Another zone serves as vanity or writing desk. A wonderful, painted wardrobe has its own corner. Even the bed is distinctly divided into two zones marked by pillows and pictures over the double headboard. *Courtesy of Hotel Byblos.*

Here's the next best thing to camping out in winter: a two-wall mural of the snow-dusted Rockies, complete with indoor plumbing and heat. Look for wildlife hiding in the woods without leaving your bed. *Courtesy of Capitol Hill Mansion*

A whimsical stretch of picket fence capped by birdhouses, a bright floral bedspread over a plaid skirt, and lovely lavender walls – this room is the happy creation of a decorator who likes to play. *Courtesy of Five Gables Inn & Spa*

Chapter 9

FEMININE FLAIR

In the human species it is, with many exceptions, the woman who feathers the nest. The woman who hangs up all the pretty elements, on herself and in the house, to attract a mate, and to make the place so comfortable her family feels like sticking around. She leaves her mark with lace and flowers, fresh linens and other finery. Courtesy of Whitegate Inn Bed & Breakfast.

A fishnet canopy covers this luxurious king-size bed. Two wing chairs dominate the sitting area, and original artworks grace the walls. *Courtesy of Waterloo Country Inn.*

A handsomely crafted bed takes center stage amidst a cast of rich pinks and greens. Resisting the natural inclination to center everything, this decorator moved one lovely piece of art into a corner above the fireplace. *Courtesy of Whitegate Inn Bed & Breakfast.*

Furnished with wonderful antiques, including the painted brass bed and a daybed in the foreground, this room is tied together by a sunny floral bedspread, curtains, and border paper. *Courtesy of Cameo Rose Victorian Country Inn.*

A bedroom is all about textiles – the warm, or smooth, or fuzzy fabrics in which we wrap ourselves for sleep. Here a pleasing mix of white linens with splashes of quilted color. *Courtesy of Rabbit Hill Inn.*

Feminine pinks and florals stripe the walls and dot a lovely pieced quilt. This room is replete with small touches – a pillow becomes a gift with a white bow, a soft rabbit offers to share a chair, antique luggage and a hat announce that you've arrived. *Courtesy of Rabbit Hill Inn.*

An unusual patchwork-style Oriental carpet adds color and character to a wonderful room draped in white. *Courtesy of The Log House & Homestead.*

This is a small room, so compact furniture was required, and every foot of available space was utilized. The delicate size of the table lamps adds stature to the bed and its side tables. The colors in the floral bedspread and curtain were repeated in a stenciled arc over the headboard. *Courtesy of Holly Hedge House.*

Rich mauves and pinks create a romantic space, complete with working fireplace. A brightly lit alcove is dedicated to morning primping. *Courtesy of The Hillcrest Inn.*

131

A woodstove not only adds historic charm to a room, it makes it incredibly cozy even on the coldest of nights. *Courtesy of Victoria's Keep.*

A feminine touch is evidenced in floral bedspread and pastel pink walls draped with chiffon. Much of this room's charm is owing to the four-poster bed constructed in front porch style with the illusion of wooden balusters and columns, complemented by a wicker wardrobe. *Courtesy of A Victorian on the Bay.*

Check out these grand windows, or check out underneath them. What a view to wake up to, and it hasn't been obscured by excessive window treatments – just lightly draped in the sheerest of lace. *Courtesy of A Victorian on the Bay.*

The lavender and green decor tie in with a stenciled ceiling border of wisteria. The small arched windows are built into panels of the original cherry woodwork. *Courtesy of Capitol Hill Mansion.*

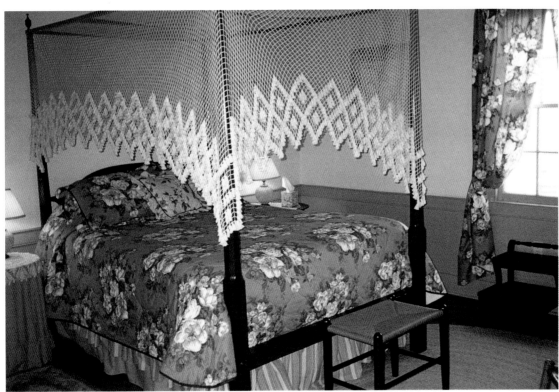

This room has been kept simple, with a basic green and gold color scheme accented by white in the textiles and bed canopy. *Courtesy of Edgewood Farm.*

A palette of whites gives this room its fresh, feminine feel. Positioning the bed in the corner allowed for wall-mounted side tables, each graced with elegant lighting. *Courtesy of Cumberland Falls Bed and Breakfast Inn.*

Crested wallpaper, carved antique furnishings, and a canopied bed create a genteel, romantic room. *Courtesy of Hennessey House.*

Green wallpaper panels are foil for a floral chintz duvet quilt and matching window treatments. *Courtesy of Henley House.*

Rose paint works with rose wallpaper and bedspread is this charming room. *Courtesy of Hennessey House.*

Blues work together to create a flower-starred nightscape. *Courtesy of Hennessey House.*

Tassels fringe the overlapping blue and gold canopies that turn this bed into a conversation piece. *Courtesy of Monmouth Plantation.*

Pink valance and curtains hang like elaborate hats over the windows in this maidenly room. *Courtesy of Monmouth Plantation.*

Lacy yellow curtains and bed canopy imitate an elaborate wallpaper border below the ceiling. Marble in fireplace surround and the table add earthly weight to this fairy tale room. *Courtesy of Monmouth Plantation.*

Lace overlays a pink bedspread, creating an effect similar to the elaborate print in the room's textiles. *Courtesy of Monmouth Plantation.*

Yellow adds sunshine to a room rich in dark wooden antiques. *Courtesy of Monmouth Plantation.*

Strawberry and cream tones fill this delicious room, from the puddling textiles to the wonderful wallpaper scenes set in frames of fancy millwork. *Courtesy of Monmouth Plantation.*

Satiny pink brocade is trimmed in blue for this his-n-hers room. An elaborately carved antique, four-poster bed terminates in claw feet and two wonderful antique end tables stand as one-of-a-kind testaments to taste. *Courtesy of Monmouth Plantation.*

Tasseled draperies form a two-toned scallop around the bed and window in an elaborate interplay of pink and blue. *Courtesy of Monmouth Plantation.*

A beautiful, carved mantel surrounds a stone and brick fireplace in this romantic little getaway. Three big windows are delicately draped in lace for privacy and romantic effect. *Courtesy of Monmouth Plantation.*

Yards and yards of satin brocade went into creating this matching set of bed and window treatments. *Courtesy of Monmouth Plantation.*

The golden hues of knotty pine furniture are complemented b a two-tone yellow an white room. A recessed fireplace is the room's center-piece. And here's a great idea for a little extra storage space - box alongside the fo of the bed, space that's rarely used. *Courtesy of Lilac Inn*

Fluffy white linens and white furnishings create a private cloud, contrasted with muted lichen colored walls. *Courtesy of Oakland House Seaside Resort.*

Blue is a relaxing color, whether found in the sky, the sea, or the bedroom. Here elegant draperies fringe a canopied bed. The color is picked up in the brocade chair upholstery, window treatments, and quilt. *Courtesy of Rabbit Hill Inn.*

A cheerful floral cotton was chosen for coordinated bed ruffle, pillows, and elegant window treatments. The ceiling-to-floor curtains echo the vertical lines in the wallpaper – both emphasizing the high ceiling. *Courtesy of Hotel Jerome.*

An antique wash basin and mirror grace one corner, the bed dominates another in this sunny room. *Courtesy of The Mill Brook.*

Floral curtains over the windows and botanical prints over the bed bring a cheerful, feminine atmosphere to this room. *Courtesy of The Breakers.*

Custom upholstery is tied in with a big throw pillow, a subtle touch in a room bright with sunny colors.
Courtesy of The Chesterfield Hotel.

A floral fantasy envelopes this king-size bed, with custom drapery and bed linens.
Courtesy of Hotel Bel-Air.

A loveseat offers a couple a fireside spot to cuddle each other, or their morning cup of coffee. Elegant details include the moldings on walls and the fireplace surround, and a fireside alcove with pedestal table and fresh flowers. *Courtesy of The Waldorf Towers.*

Mint and peach tones mingle in stripes, squares, and solids in this beautifully coordinated room. *Courtesy of The Waldorf Towers.*

A floral bedspread takes center stage in this room, curtained by satin-striped white wallpaper and set with dusty rose and green furnishings. *Courtesy of The Pierre Hotel.*

The color of cream after the strawberries have been savored, this gentle room is replete with detail, from the fringed drapes to the elaborately carved bedstead. *Courtesy of Monmouth Plantation.*

A sweeping arch over the bed is draped in lace. Underneath, quilts and comforters beckon one (or two) to snuggle in. *Courtesy of Whitegate Inn Bed & Breakfast.*

This master bedroom is made all
the more comfortable by a
fireplace and a large sitting area.
The Inn at Stockbridge.

RESOURCE GUIDE

Applewood Inn & Restaurant
13555 Highway 116
Guerneville, California 95446
707-869-9093/800-555-8509
www.applewoodinn.com
   Minutes from wineries and the rugged Sonoma Coast
in the Russian River Valley, this inn decor is notable for its
Mediterranean flavor, created using vibrant colors and a
mix of antique and contemporary furnishings.

The Artist's Inn & Gallery
P.O. Box 26
117 East Main Street
Terre Hill, Pennsylvania 17581
717-445-0219/888-999-4479
www.artistinn.com
   This 150-year old home includes modern creature
comforts like central air, whirlpool baths, and fireplaces.
Four-course candlelight breakfasts are served daily. Local
attractions include Amish country, antique and outlet
shopping, and museums.

The Ashton
610 Main Street
Fort Worth, Texas 76102
817-332-0100
www.theashtonhotel.com
   The Ashton made its debut in the spring of 2001 in an
historic building in the heart of the city. The interior
design is contemporary, marrying antique moldings with
dropped stained glass ceilings and backlit upholstered
walls.

Ashton Country House
1205 Middlebrook Avenue
Staunton, Virginia 24401
540-885-7819/800-296-7819
www.bbhost.com/ashtonbnb
   This 1860 home has a rich history that includes occu-
pation by Confederate troops shortly after it was built.
The building offers magnificent views of the Blue Ridge
Mountains, as well as pastures and a barn for adventur-
ous guests to explore.

L'Auberge Provencale
P.O. Box 190
White Post, Virginia 22663
540-837-1375/800-638-1702
www.laubergeprovencale.com
   This inn transports visitors to Southern France, where
Chef Alain Borel serves up exquisite regional cuisine from
his native Avignon and his wife, Celeste, provides warm
hospitality in exquisite surroundings. Located in Virginia
hunt country.

Begawan Giri Estate
P.O. Box 54
Ubud 80571
Bali, Indonesia
(62 361) 978888
www.begawan.com
   This private estate is set amidst Bali's stunning land-
scape, close to Ubud, Bali's creative and cultural center.
Spread out over eight hectares of lush tropical gardens,
the estate offers complete residences to the guests.

Bellevue Club Hotel
11200 Southeast 6th
Bellevue, Washington 98004
425-455-1616
www.bellevueclub.com

Set on nine and a half beautifully landscaped acres, the club offers convenient access to Seattle and surrounding areas. From the athletic facilities to the hotel, it is a warm and welcoming "home away from home" for members and guests.

Birchwood Inn
7 Hubbard Street
Lenox, Massachusetts 01240
413-637-2600/800-524-1646
www.birchwood-inn.com

This 1767 Colonial Revival mansion is in the Berkshires of Western Massachusetts, home to Shakespeare & Co., The Norman Rockwell Museum, Edith Wharton's The Mount, and Tanglewood, summer home of the Boston Symphony Orchestra.

Black Forest Inn
23191 Highway 385
Rapid City, South Dakota 57702
605-574-2000/800-888-1607
www.blackforestinn.net

Bob and Betty Barkley welcome guests to their bed and breakfast lodge for everything from corporate retreats to simple weekend getaways and family vacations. The two specialize in delicious breakfasts and home-baked cookies.

The Breakers
One South County Road
Palm Beach, Florida 33480
561-659-8403/888 273 2537
www.thebreakers.com

This Mobil Five-Star and AAA Five Diamond oceanfront resort is situated on 140 acres. The Italian Renaissance facility includes two 18-hole golf courses, a luxury spa, Mediterranean-style beach club, four swimming pools, and much more.

Cameo Rose Victorian Country Inn
1090 Severson Road
Belleville, Wisconsin 53508
608-424-6340
www.CameoRose.com

Guests enjoy immense peace, elegance, and comfort, and miles of private hiking trails This romantic bed and breakfast sets amidst the hills midway between Madison and New Glarus, Wisconsin; an area is known as America's Little Switzerland.

Capitol Hill Mansion Bed & Breakfast
1207 Pennsylvania Street
Denver, Colorado 80203
303-839-5221/800-839-9329
capitolhillmansion.com

This national registered inn borders downtown Denver on the historic East Side and has been given the Best Value Hotel by citysearch.com and the Best of Denver award by Westword Magazine.

Captain Nickerson Inn
333 Main Street
South Dennis, Massachusetts 02660
508-398-5966/800-282-1619
www.bbonline.com/ma/captnick/

On a scenic bike path in the heart of Cape Cod, this inn provides the beauty of stained glass windows, parquet floors, and antique fireplaces. The Inn was built by a sea captain in 1828, and remodeled in 1879 to its present Queen Anne style.

Casa Del Mar Inn
18 Bath Street
Santa Barbara California 93101
805-963-4418/800-433-3097
www.casadelmar.com

This charming, 21-room, Mediterranean-style inn combines the very best of a bed and breakfast inn and small hotel. It is less than a block from the beautiful beach, historic Stearns Wharf, and the yacht harbor.

Chatham Bars Inn
Shore Road, Chatham
Cape Cod, Massachusetts 02633
508-945-0096
www.chathambarsinn.com

Since that June day in 1914, when Boston stockbroker Charles Ashley Hardy officially opened the Inn, the resort has charmed and soothed the most discerning guests. Generations return year after year to savor the traditions and bask in the natural beauty.

Cheeca Lodge
P.O. Box 527
Islamorada, Florida 33036
305-664-4651
www.rockresorts.com

This 27-acre resort in the Florida Keys offers access to incredible fishing and diving, palm-lined beach, and lush gardens. The resort offers environmental programs for guests and their children, plus a spa and fitness center.

The Chesterfield Palm Beach

363 Cocoanut Row
Palm Beach, Florida 33480
561-659-5800
www.redcarnationhotels.com

Dedicated to discreet personal service and exceptional comfort for the ultimate Palm Beach experience. Within strolling distance of the exclusive shops of Worth Avenue and the Atlantic Ocean.

Chipita Lodge

9090 Chipita Park Road
Chipita Park, Colorado 80809
719-684-8454/877-Chipita
www.chipitalodge.com

At the base of Pikes Peak, this beautiful assembly of native logs and stone offers its guests an endless supply of cool mountain breezes, a soak in the hot tub under the stars, or relaxing before a roaring fire in the gathering room.

Cincinnati's Weller Haus Bed and Breakfast

319 Poplar Street
Newport, Kentucky 41073
859-431-6829/800-431-4287
www.wellerhaus.com

The charm of the 1880s lingers in this Preservation Awarded bed and breakfast listed on the National Register of Historic Places, featuring original millwork and eighteenth century period pieces.

The Columns on Alamo

1037 South Alamo
San Antonio, Texas 78210
210-271-3245/800-233-3364
www.bbonline.com/tx/columns

A bed and breakfast established in 1994 by Ellenor and Art Link in their gracious 1892 Greek Revival home and the adjacent 1901 guest house. Thirteen guest rooms are furnished with comfortable Victorian antiques and period reproductions.

Cumberland Falls Bed and Breakfast Inn

254 Cumberland Avenue
Asheville, North Carolina 28801
828-253-4085/888-743-2557
www.cumberlandfalls.com

This quiet inn greets guests with a waterfall, koi ponds, and lily pads in a lush garden. Fresh flowers and homemade baked treats, and a gourmet, four-course candlelight breakfast are among the indoor amenities.

The Dharmawangsa

Jalan Brawijaya Raya, No 26
Jakarta
Indonesia 12160
62.21.725.8181
www.rosewoodhotels.com

Here guests are received as honored visitors to a spacious, private residence. *Set* amidst the leafy quarters of Jakarta's most fashionable residential area, Kebayoran Baru, The Dharmawangsa is the epitome of classic Javanese style.

The Dupont at the Circle

1604 19th Street, NW
Washington, D.C. 20009
202-332-5251/888-412-0100
www.dupontatthecircle.com

An urban bed and breakfast inn located in the heart of the nation's capital, consisting of two completely restored Victorian townhouses, combining the charm of yesteryear with modern conveniences. The seven guest rooms and two-room suite are appointed with antique furniture and sumptuous linens.

Edgewood Farm Bed & Breakfast

1186 Middle River Road
Stanardsville, Virginia 22973
804-985-3782/800-985-3782
www.edgewoodfarmbandb.com

On a secluded 130-acre farm in the foothills of the Blue Ridge, this 1790 home has been faithfully restored. Guests enjoy wildflower and perennial gardens, as well as nearby attractions including Skyline Drive, Charlottesville, and vineyards.

The Equinox

Historic Route 7A
Manchester Village, Vermont 05254
802-362-4700/800-362-4747
www.equinoxresort.com
Encompassing breathtaking mountain views, this historic luxury resort is a wonderful rest stop between outdoor activities. More than 183 guest rooms are furnished with antiques and richly textured fabrics.

The Fairmont Scottsdale Princess

7575 East Princess Drive
Scottsdale, Arizona, 85255
480-585-4848
www.scottsdaleprincess.com
This ultimate desert oasis is one of the Leading Hotels of the World and a AAA Five Diamond Resort. Guests enjoy two 18 hole golf courses, three swimming pools, seven tennis courts, a spa and fitness center, and more.

Fifteen Beacon
15 Beacon Street
Boston, Massachusetts 02108
617-670-1500/877-982-3226
www.xvbeacon.com
  Opened in January 2000, Fifteen Beacon is a refined landmark hotel in a 1903 Beaux-Arts building that juxtaposes cutting-edge technology with extraordinary Jeffersonian styling.

Five Gables Inn & Spa
209 N. Talbot Street
St. Michaels, Maryland 21663
410-745-0100/877-466-0100
www.fivegables.com
  Sixteen incomparably charming rooms provide meditative resting places between hydrotherapy treatments, facials, and massage.

Franklin Manor Bed & Breakfast
627 W. Colorado Avenue
Telluride, Colorado 81435
970-728-4241/888-728-3351
www.franklinmanor.com
  Specializing in romantic getaways, the innkeepers emphasize whirlpool tubs for two, fireplaces, private balconies, gourmet breakfasts, and afternoon wine tastings. Franklin Manor and Gallery are named after the late neo-classical artist Richard Franklin.

Gaige House Inn
13540 Arnold Drive
Glen Ellen, California 95442
707-935-0237/800-935-0237
www.gaige.com
  This luxury inn features fifteen guest rooms in an 1890 Queen Anne-Italianate building that enjoys continued renovation and improvements. The sophisticated interior decor fuses Asian and Indonesian influences with re-strained California simplicity.

Grand Hotel Excelsior Vittoria
Piazza Tasso, 34
80067 Sorrento (Naples)
Italy
+39 081-807 1044
www.exvitt.it
  This five-star hotel has 95 panoramic rooms and 16 suites, with a terrace or a balcony facing the Gulf of Naples or the five acres orange grove surrounding the hotel. The antique suites are tastefully furnished with original period furniture.

Henley House Bed and Breakfast
1025 8th Avenue
New West Minster, British Columbia
Canada V3M 2R5
604-526-3919
www.henleyhouse.com
A lovely and colorful garden is the setting for this handsome 1925 Craftsman style home conveniently located in the Greater Vancouver area of British Columbia.

Hennessey House
1727 Main Street
Napa, California 94559
707-226-3774
www.hennesseyhouse.com
  The Hennessey House is known as Napa's 1889 Queen Anne Victorian Bed and Breakfast. Guests are invited to watch the sun rise over the mountains from the front porch and sip wine and share conversation by the fountain.

The Hillcrest Inn
540 Storle Avenue
Burlington, Wisconsin 53105
262-763-4706/800-313-9030
www.thehillcrestinn.com
  Nestled on the shores of Echo Lake and the Fox and White Rivers, this four-acre, 1908 estate offers a multitude of outdoor recreational activities and is located within minutes of a downtown rich in antique and retail stores, art galleries, and restaurants.

Holly Hedge House Bed & Breakfast Cottage
908 Grant Avenue South
Renton, Washington 98055
425-226-2555/888-226-2555
www.nwlink.com/~holihedg/
  This private, award-winning cottage is nestled atop a scenic hill. It is located within walking distance of antique shops, restaurants, walking and biking trails, and outdoor water sports on the Cedar River.

Hotel Bel-Air
701 Stone Canyon Boulevard
Los Angeles, California 90077
310-472-1211/800-648-4097
www.hotelbelair.com
  This 11-acre enclave near Beverly Hills and Sunset Boulevard was designed as a California oasis. It has played host to privacy seeking celebrities including Grace Kelly, Jackie Gleason, Cary Grant, Elizabeth Taylor, and Marilyn Monroe.

Hotel Byblos
Avenue Paul Signac
83990 Saint-Tropez
France
33 (0) 4 94 56 68 00
www.byblos.com
  Interpreting traditional Provencal style to elegant and luxurious accommodations in the heart of the most mythical seaside resort on the Côte d'Azur.

Hotel Byblos des Neiges
BP 98 - 73122 Courchevel Cedex
France
33 (0) 4 79 00 98 00
www.byblos.com
  Located at the foot of the largest ski area in the world in the French Alps, this authentic mountain chalet envelopes guests in a world of luxury and sophistication.

Hotel de l'Europe
Nieuwe Doelenstraat 2-8
1012 CP Amsterdam
The Netherlands
(+31) 20 5311777
www.leurope.nl
  Right in the heart of old Amsterdam is one of the "Leading Hotels of the World." Guests are surrounded by the luxuries of classical splendor, and up-to-date comfort. The hotel and its site have a lush history of hospitality, spanning back to the 1400s.

Hotel Jerome
330 East Main Street
Aspen, Colorado 81611
970-920-1000/800-331-7213
www.hoteljerome.com
  Voted one of The Ten Best Ski Hotels by Ski Magazine, the hotel offers 93 spacious rooms and suites. Listed in the National Register of Historic Places, the hotel is renowned for its tradition of Aspen elegance and gracious hospitality.

Hotel Lancaster
7, rue de Berri
75008 Paris
France
(33) 1 40 76 40 76
www.hotel-lancaster.fr
  Located within walking distance of the Champs Elysées and the Arc de Triomphe, this five-star hotel has 50 rooms and 10 suites, all decorated in period style with original antiques, silk fabrics, Braquenié carpets, Porthault linens, and original oil paintings.

Hotel Le Bristol
112 re du Faubourg St. Honoré
75008 Paris
France
(33) 153 43 43 00
www.hotel-bristol.com
  Located near the Presidential Palace and steps from the Champs-Elysées Gardens, the hotel has 178 rooms, each uniquely decorated in luxurious chintz fabrics and rare antiques. Additionally there are more than 35,000 square feet of gardens.

Hotel Maison de Ville
727 Rue Toulouse
New Orleans, Louisiana 70130
504-561-5858/800-634-1600
www.maisondeville.com
  In the heart of the French Quarter, this member of Historic Hotels of America is furnished with rare antiques and period paintings. The hotel and its Audubon Cottages are clustered around a pristine swimming pool.

Hôtel Plaza Athénée
37 East 64th Street at Madison Avenue
New York, New York 10021
212-734-9100/800-447-8800
www.plaza-athenee.com
  Nestled on a quiet, tree-lined street in the heart of one of the busiest cities in the world, this charming, European-style hotel is but a brief stroll to boutiques, galleries, museums, and Central Park.

Hotel Santa Caterina
Via SS. Amalfitana
9 - 84011 Amalfi (SA)
Italy
+39.89.871012
www.hotelsantacaterina.it
  This white mansion is perched on a cliff lush with Mediterranean vegetation and lemon groves. Elevators carved into the cliff deliver guests to the beach below. The hotel has been owned and managed by one family since 1904.

Hotel Sausalito
16 El Portal
Sausalito, California 94965
415-332-0700/888-442-0700
www.hotelsausalito.com
  This Mission Revival Style boutique hotel is steeped in history, and started its days (circa 1915) as a bordello. It faces Historic Vina Del Mar Park and is only steps from the Sausalito harbor and many galleries and boutiques.

Hotel Vier Jahreszeiten
Neuer Jungfernstieg 9-14
20354 Hamburg
Germany
+49 40-34940
www.hvj.de

Prominently located on the western side of the inner Alster Lake shore, Hotel Vier Jahreszeiten lies in the heart of the prime retail and commercial district. Founded in 1897, the hotel has been consistently ranked among the top hotels in the world.

The Inn at Essex
70 Essex Way
Essex Junction, Vermont 05452
802-878-1100/800-727-4295
www.innatessex.com

A splendid, 120-room Colonial-style inn where guest rooms and suites are perfectly appointed with period reproduction furniture and handsome draperies and linens.

The Inn at 410
410 North Leroux Street
Flagstaff, Arizona 86001
520-774-0088/800-774-2008
www.inn410.com

A gourmet breakfast in the morning and home-baked cookies at the end of the day are features of this bed and breakfast. It is located just blocks from historic downtown Flagstaff and within an easy drive to Grand Canyon National Park.

The Inn at Irving Place
56 Irving Place
New York, New York 10003
212-533-4600
www.InnatIrving.com

In the heart of New York's historical Gramercy Park, these 1834 landmark townhouses have been meticulously transformed to recreate a bygone era of gracious living, while offering personalized service and amenities.

The Inn at Stockbridge
Route 7 Box 618
Stockbridge, Massachusetts 01262
413-298-3337
www.stockbridgeinn.com

This 1906 Georgian-style mansion is on 12 secluded acres in the heart of the Berkshires of Western Massachusetts, one of America's premier cultural destinations. The inn has 12 well-appointed guest rooms as well as large common rooms.

Joshua Grindle Inn
P.O. Box 647
Mendocino, California 95460
707-937-4143/800-grindle
www.joshgrin.com

This inn was furnished with owner Jim and Arlene's personal collection of antiques featuring Early American and shaker era pieces. The rooms are light and airy and have comfortably arranged seating areas.

Kahala Mandarin Oriental
5000 Kahala Avenue
Honolulu, Hawaii 96816
808-739-888
www.mandarin-oriental.com

Guest rooms recall the feel of a grand Hawaiian plantation home in generous proportions and sumptuous comfort. The romantic ambiance is a handsome mixture of mahogany furniture, teak parquet floors, and a blend of rich fabrics.

Kempinski Hotel Corvinus
Erzsébet tér 7-8
1051 Budapest
Hungary
+36-1-429-3777
www.kempinski-budapest.com

This luxury hotel was recently redecorated by Ágnes Bálint to evoke the renaissance world of King Matthias Corvinus while maintaining the empire style of the hotel. The hotel has housed many celebrities and world figures.

The Lancaster
701 Texas Avenue at Louisiana
Houston, Texas 77002
713-228-9500/800-231-0336
www.lancaster.com

Guests experience a transformation from the city's clamor to intimate and quiet comfort. The atmosphere is reminiscent of an English country manor, with 18th century art, fine antique furniture, and fresh floral arrangements.

The Lanesborough
Hyde Park Corner
London, SW1X7TA
England
+44 20.7259.5599/800-999-1828
www.rosewoodhotels.com

The Lanesborough captures the gracious style and warm hospitality of an early 19th-century residence. Ideally located on Hyde Park Corner, this 1828 landmark building has been meticulously restored to its original grandeur.

Lilac Inn
53 Park Street
Brandon, Vermont 05733
802-247-5463/800-221-0720
www.lilacinn.com

This 1909 Greek Revival mansion was once a summer "cottage" to financier Albert Farr, and now is a vacation home for many. In 1993, Michael Shane opened the home as an inn after two years of extensive renovations.

Litchfield Plantation
P.O. Box 290
Pawleys Island, South Carolina 29585
843-237-9121/800-869-1410
www.litchfieldplantation.com

This extraordinary retreat is located on the principal 600 acres of a 1750s South Carolina coastal rice plantation. It was meticulously transformed into a country inn combining historic flavor with modern amenities.

The Lodge & Spa at Breckenridge
112 Overlook Drive
P.O. Box 1078
Breckenridge, Colorado 80424
970-453-9300/800-736-1607
www.thelodgeatbreck.com

Nestled on a magnificent forested cliff, five minutes from the town of Breckenridge is the Lodge and Spa at Breckenridge. The upscale hotel is an intimate retreat featuring a full-service spa and elegant guest rooms with spectacular mountain views.

The Log House & Homestead on Spirit Lake
P.O. Box 130
Vergas, Minnesota 56587
218-342-2318/800-342-2318
www.loghousebb.com

Overlooking Spirit Lake near Vergas, Minnesota , the Log House and Homestead Bed and Breakfast is cradled amidst 115 acres of hills, fields and maple woods in the heart of the famous Minnesota lake country. Luxury and pampering are its hallmark.

The Madison Hotel
Fifteenth & M Streets NW
Washington, D.C. 20005
202-862-1600/800-424-8577
www.themadisonhotel.net

Just four blocks from the White House, The Madison routinely plays host to Presidents, Heads of State, and Fortune 500 CEOs.

Mandarin Oriental * Hotel du Rhône
Quai Turrettini
Case postale 2040
1211 Geneva
Switzerland
(41) 22 909 0000
www.mandarinoriental.com

For the past 50 years, this hotel has been Geneva's best address for business and leisure, offering guests a world of refined elegance and outstanding service.

Mandarin Oriental * Hyde Park
66 Knightsbridge
London SW1X 7LA
England
(44) 020 7235 2000
www.mandarinoriental.com

The residence of the cream of British society in 1892, now it serves a sophisticated public, only a sovereign's throw from Hyde Park, Harvey Nichols, Harrod's, and the boutiques of Sloane Street.

Mandarin Oriental * San Francisco
222 Sansome Street
San Francisco, California 94104
415-276-9888
www.mandarin-oriental.com

The city's only Mobil Five-Star luxury hotel occupies the top eleven floors of the city's third tallest building, offering breathtaking views from above, and easy walking to Union Square, shopping, the theater district, Chinatown, and cable car lines.

The Mark
Madison Avenue at East 77th Street
New York, New York 10021
212-744-4300
www.mandarinoriental.com

The Mark is New York's casual luxury hotel, minutes from midtown and a complimentary shuttle ride from the Wall Street area; mere steps from the world's most exclusive shopping, Museum Mile, and Central Park.

Le Meridien Sydney
11 Jamison Street
Sydney NSW 2000
Australia
(61-2) 9696 2620
www.lemeridien-sydney.com

Le Meridien Sydney presents a luxurious 415-room hotel, combining five-star hospitality, Australian culture, and European style. It is located in the heart of the business and shopping district.

The Merrion Dublin
Upper Merrion Street
Dublin 2
Ireland
353 1 603 0600
www.merrionhotel.com
   This luxury hotel is arranged around two private, 18th century-style gardens. The interior uses 18th century colors, antiques, and furniture and fabric styles, and houses one of Ireland's largest private collections of art including works by 20th century Irish artists.

The Mill Brook Bed & Breakfast
P.O. Box 410 Route 44
Brownsville, Vermont 05037
802-484-7283
www.millbrookbb.com
   This charming bed and breakfast is located in the heart of a town famous for baked beans suppers. The house is steeped in history, dating back to Jacob Sykes, patriarch of a family run hardwood lumber mill.

Monmouth Plantation
36 Melrose Avenue
Natchez, Mississippi 39120
601-442-5852/800-828-4531
www.monmouthplantation.com
   This award-winning Greek Revival mansion was built in 1818, and has been lovingly restored and furnished with antiques and lavish details. It features thirty-one beautifully appointed rooms, 26 acres of walking trails and gardens, and gourmet Southern cuisine.

Oakland House Seaside Resort
435 Herrick Road
Brooksville, Maine 04617
207-359-8521/800-359-Relax
www.oaklandhouse.com
   Secluded on 50 acres of prime oceanfront. Today, Jim Littlefield carries on the innkeeping that his great-grandfather started in 1889. The same sign that welcomed 19th century visitors who arrived by coastal steamboat at Herrick's Landing, still greets visitors today.

The Oberoi
Medana Beach, P.O. Box 1096
Mataram 83001
Lombok, N.T.B.
Indonesia
(62-370) 638-444
www.lhw.com/oberoilomb
   Lombok, the unspoiled island neighboring Bali in the archipelago of Indonesia, is rich in lush rainforest, golden beaches, coral, and tropical fish. This 24-acre resort offers a choice of villas and terrace pavilions built in the style of a native village.

Old Monterey Inn
500 Martin Street
Monterey, California 93940
831-375-8284/800-350-2344
www.oldmontereyinn.com
   This ivy covered Tudor-style residence was built in 1929 and to this day maintains most of its original architectural elements, including stained glass windows. Contemporary skylights in combination with period furniture and family antiques evoke romance.

On the Banks of the Everglades
201 West Broadway
Everglades City, Florida 34139
941-695-3335/888-431-1977
www.banksoftheeverglades.com
   Millionaire railroad man and speculator Barron G. Collier erected this grand bank building in 1923. He also founded Everglades City, convinced that it would one day rival Miami in size. Today the bank is a bed and breakfast in the heart of a sleepy, tropical fishing village.

The Oriental Singapore
5 Raffles Avenue
Marina Square
Singapore 039797
(65) 338 0066
www.mandarinoriental.com
   The Oriental is Singapore's only Mandarin Oriental hotel, combining spectacular architectural design with a superior standard of comfort and service.

Palisades Bed & Breakfast at Dash Point
5162 Southwest 311th Place
Federal Way, Washington 98023
253-838-4376/888-838-4376
www.bbonline.com/wa/palisades
   A private, serene, and comfortable home with a breath-taking view of Puget Sound and the Olympic mountain Range. Guests enjoy a private English garden and a sandy waterfront beach for strolling, great breakfasts, and general pampering.

The Pan Pacific San Francisco
500 Post Street at Union Square
San Francisco, California 94102
415-771-8600/800-327-8585
www.panpac.com
   Taking pride in the countless details inside, the Pan Pacific sends its pampered guests out to the bustle of Union Square and San Francisco's business and financial centers, the theater district, and Chinatown.

The Peninsula New York
700 Fifth Avenue at 55th Street
New York, New York 10019
212-956-2888/800-262-9467
www.peninsula.com
   Housed in a landmark building constructed in 1905, this 23-story hotel is a classic example of Beaux Arts architecture. Completely renovated in 1998, all of the rooms feature period reproduction furniture with contemporary fabrics.

Philip Porcher House
19 Archdale Street
Charleston, South Carolina 29401
843-722-1801
www.bbonline.com/sc/porcher
   This circa 1770 Georgian house is in the heart of the Historic District, within easy walking distance of the antique district, fine restaurants, shops, and museums. The guest apartment is furnished with eighteenth century engravings and period antiques.

The Pierre Hotel
Fifth Avenue at 61st Street
New York, New York 10021
212-838-8000
www.fourseasons.com
   Located across the street from Central Park, this famed landmark is a destination in itself. Enjoy a classic afternoon tea beneath the colorful trompe l'oeil ceiling in the Rotunda, or the romantic experience of dinner in the acclaimed Café Pierre.

The President's Quarters
225 East President Street
Savannah, Georgia 31401
912-233-1600/888-592-1812
www.presidentsquarters.com
   In 1987, after housing many prominent citizens of Savannah, these townhouses were carefully restored as the President's Quarters Inn. This elegant inn offers antique and period furnishings in rooms with ceilings up to 13 feet high.

Rabbit Hill Inn
48 Lower Waterford Road
Lower Waterford, Vermont 05848
802-748-5168/800-762-8669
www.rabbithillinn.com
   This elegant, 200-year-old inn sits in the storybook White Village in Vermont's Northeast Kingdom. The innkeepers offer award-winning gourmet cuisine, and outdoor activities for all seasons including acres of walking trails and gardens, swimming, canoeing, and skiing.

Reid's Palace Hotel
Estrada Monumental 139
9000-098 Funchal
Madeira
Portugal
Tel: +351 291 71 71 71
www.reidspalace.orient-express.com
   Set on the cliff top in ten acres of tropical gardens overlooking the Bay of Funchal and the Atlantic, Reid's Palace Hotel has, for over 100 years, been a standard-bearer for excellence in Madeira and beyond.

The Ritz, London
150 Piccadilly
London W1V 9DG
England
+44 (020) 7300 2308/877-748-9536
www.theritzhotel.co.uk
   Built in the style of a French chateau, the hotel has a series of elegant public and private rooms, combined with many beautiful suites, some overlooking Green Park. The Ritz has a guest to staff ratio of 2:1 and, needless to say, 24-hour service.

Rose Inn
813 Auburn Road, Route 34
Ithaca, New York 14851
607-533-7905
www.roseinn.com
   This Italianate mansion, known locally as "the House with the Circular Staircase" was built on 20 acres in hilly countryside ten miles north of Ithaca. The bed and breakfast has 20 guestrooms including 10 deluxe suites complete with fireplaces and whirlpool tubs.

Le Royal Meridien Baan
   Taling Ngam in Koh Samui
Two Pacific Place
17th Floor, Suite 1702
142 Sukhamvit Road
Bangkok 10110
Thailand
662-653-2201
www.lemeridien.co.th
www.lemeridien-hotels.com
   Guest rooms and suites feature Thai architecture with a blend of natural materials and traditional motifs.

Sampson Eagon Inn
238 East Beverley Street
Staunton, Virginia 24401
540-886-8200/800-597-9722
www.eagoninn.com
   This gracious, lovingly restored antebellum mansion, circa 1840, is located in the beautiful Shenandoah Valley and in the heart of historic Staunton's beautifully restored Victorian downtown.

Sanctuary on Camelback Mountain
5700 East McDonald Drive
Paradise Valley, Arizona 85253
480-948-2100
www.theatlantichotel.com/pages/s/scogara.html
   This magnificent destination spa provides therapies culled from East and West in state-of-the-art facilities in a desert setting. Guests stay in zen-like casita guest rooms and suites terraced into the slopes.

Southwest Inn at Sedona
3250 West Highway 89A
Sedona, Arizona 86336
520-282-3344/800-483-7422
www.swinn.com
   Set amidst spectacular red rock vistas, near stunning canyons and ancient Indian ruins, innkeepers Joel and Sheila Gilgoff offer a place to relax after rugged outdoor adventure. This small, luxury hotel has the AAA Four Diamond Award.

Thurnhers Alpenhof
A-6763 Zuers am Arlberg
Austria
+43 55 83-21 91
www.thurnhers-alpenhof.at
   Situated in one of the country's most exclusive winter sports resorts, the Zuers am Arlberg is a welcoming combination of family traditions, luxury and utmost hospitality.

Las Ventanas al Paraiso
KM 19.5 Carretera Transpeninsular
San Jose del Cabo
Baja California Sur 23400
Los Cabos
Mexico
   Lying between sapphire seas and painted desert sands, rough-hewn mountains and golden beaches, this luxurious resort offers exquisite style an ambiance as warm as the Mexican sun. Lavishly vast rooms and public areas reflect the region's traditional architecture.

The Veranda Inn
38 Prospect Avenue
Eureka Springs, Arkansas 72632
501-253-7292/888-295-2171
www.theverandainn.com
   A National Register Landmark Mansion in an enchanting Ozark mountain village, this 1889 Colonial Revival mansion was designed by the famous architect, Theodore Link. A full gourmet breakfast is served on the veranda or in the dining room.

A Victorian on the Bay
57 South Bay Avenue
Eastport, New York 11941
516-325-1000/888-449-0620
www.victorianonthebay.com
   A seashore retreat located only an hour and a half from Manhattan, this is a brand new structure designed from the ground up to be a modern escape in traditional Victorian style.

Victoria's Keep
202 Ruxton Avenue
Manitou Springs, Colorado 80829
719-685-5354/800-905-5337
www.victoriaskeep.com
   This restored 1892 Queen Anne Victorian is surrounded by trees, with a small stream bubbling across the front yard. Guests enjoy a cozy retreat and comfortable atmosphere filled with charm, history, lovely decor, antiques, quilts, and collectibles.

Vila Vita Parc
Apartado 196 P
8365-911 Armacão de Pêra
Algarve
Portugal
(282) 31 01 00
www.vilavita.com
   This seaside resort hotel offers guests a tropical retreat, resplendent with palm trees and resort amenities. It is a member of the Leading Hotels of the World

Villa D'Este
22012 Cernobbio
Lago di Como
Italy
+39 (31) 348.1
www.villadeste.it
   This hotel has been a luxury resort for over 125 years. The site includes, among many amenities, a golf course, amazing gardens, a Turkish bath and fitness center, and a unique heated pool that floats on the one of the world's favorite lakes.

The Waldorf Towers
100 East 50th Street
New York, New York 10022
212-355-3100
www.waldorf-towers.com
   This boutique hotel occupies the 28th through 42nd floors of the Waldorf-Astoria, with a separate, dedicated entrance and lobby. It is the preferred New York residence of heads-of-state, royalty, celebrities, and corporate moguls.

Waterloo Country Inn
28822 Mt. Vernon Road
Princess Anne, Maryland 21853
410-651-0883
www.waterloocountryinn.com
   Step back in time at this elegant, beautifully restored jewel from the 1750s. The inn features antique furnishings and Victorian style.

Whitegate Inn Bed & Breakfast
499 Howard Street
Mendocino, California 95460
707-937-4892/800-531-7282
www.whitegateinn.com
   Innkeepers George and Carol Bechtloff serve up European hospitality amidst meticulously restored Victorian architecture, surrounded by gorgeous gardens and views of the rugged Pacific Coast.

Woodstock Inn & Resort
Fourteen the Green
Woodstock, Vermont 05091
802-457-1100/800-448-7900
www.woodstockinn.com
   The Woodstock Inn & Resort is a member of Small Luxury Hotels of the World and is consistently ranked among the finest hotels in the world.